MANCHESTER CITY

THE OFFICIAL ANNUAL 2022

D1477193

g

A Grange Publication

© 2021 Published by Grange Communications Ltd., Edinburgh, under licence from Manchester City Football Club. Printed in the EU.

Every effort has been made to ensure the accuracy of information within this publication but the publishers cannot be held responsible for any errors or omissions. Views expressed are those of the author and do not necessarily represent those of the publishers or the football club. All rights reserved.

Edited by David Clayton
Designed by Simon Thorley
Photographs © Man City (thanks to Victoria Haydn/Tom Flathers/Matt McNulty) and Getty Images

ISBN: 978-1-913578-77-0

CONTENTS

CHAMPIONS AGAIN!
THE 2020/21 SEASON:

SEPTEMBER

City's season started later than other clubs due to the restructured Champions League format. A tough test away to Wolves was the first match, but City showed no signs of tiredness with a sparkling first-half performance that saw a Kevin De Bruyne penalty and a Phil Foden goal give the Blues a 2-0 lead at the break.

Wolves were better after half-time and pulled one back through Jiménez, but a Gabriel Jesus strike deep into added time sealed a 3-1 win for Pep Guardiola's side.

A 2-1 Carabao Cup win over Bournemouth followed, but the next Premier League fixture with Leicester was something of a shock to the system as City were hammered 5-2 at the Etihad, conceding three penalties during a torrid 90 minutes.

City rounded the month off with a 3-0 Carabao Cup win over Burnley, with the Leicester result still fresh in the memory.

Summary:
Played: 4 Won: 3
Drawn: 0 Lost: 1
Goals for: 10
Goals against: 7

OCTOBER

A hard-earned 1-1 draw away to Leeds United – where new signing Ruben Dias made an impressive debut - kick-started October before there was a two week international break.

City returned with a 1-0 win over Arsenal – Raheem Sterling scoring the winner – before the Champions League campaign began with a 3-1 win over Porto at the Etihad with Sergio Aguero, Ilkay Gundogan and Ferran Torres all on target.

Another 1-1 draw followed away to West Ham United, with Foden levelling for City, meaning the Blues had taken just eight points from a possible 15 and were in mid-table.

Another Champions League victory – 3-0 away to Marseille – was followed by a narrow 1-0 win away to Sheffield United, with boyhood Blades fan Kyle Walker grabbing the winner.

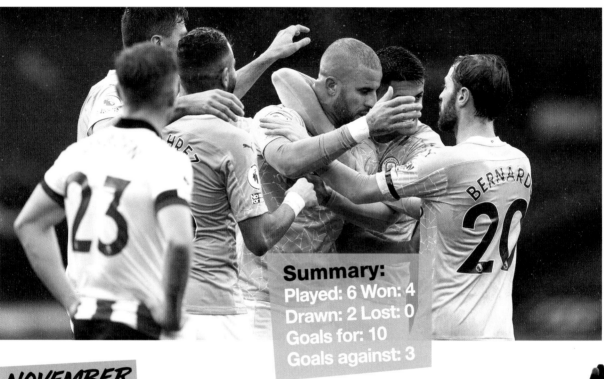

Summary:
Played: 6 Won: 4
Drawn: 2 Lost: 0
Goals for: 10
Goals against: 3

NOVEMBER

City started November by making light work of Olympiacos in the Champions League, beating the Greeks 3-0 at the Etihad.

But City's stuttering Premier League form continued, with Jesus' first-half goal earning a 1-1 home draw with champions Liverpool and De Bruyne missing a penalty just before the break.

Then, a disappointing 2-0 loss to Spurs saw Guardiola's men drop to 11th in the table – but that defeat would be the turning point in City's stop/start campaign so far.

City then secured a Round of 16 slot in the Champions League after beating Olympiacos 1-0, before thrashing Burnley 5-0 at the Etihad in the Premier League – Riyad Mahrez scored a hat-trick – to end the month positively.

Summary:
Played: 5 Won: 3
Drawn: 1 Lost: 1
Goals for: 10
Goals against: 3

DECEMBER

December was a packed but highly enjoyable month.

It began with a niggly 0-0 draw away to Porto in the Champions League and was followed by a comfortable 2-0 win over Fulham in the Premier League.

The final UCL group stage game was another comfortable win for City who beat Marseille 3-0 at the Etihad to win the group by three points. The first Manchester derby proved a cagey, tepid affair with the 0-0 draw at Old Trafford followed by a disappointing 1-1 home draw with struggling West Brom.

But City ended December on a high, with three successive wins – first a scrappy 1-0 win away to Southampton, with Sterling's 16th-minute winner enough to settle the clash at St Mary's.

Then City were at their stylish best to see off Arsenal and book a place in the Carabao Cup semi-finals, after a 4-1 win at the Emirates.

Finally, after an incredibly difficult year for everyone, and matches still being played behind closed doors, City saw off 2020 with a 2-0 win over Newcastle United on Boxing Day – Ilkay Gundogan and Torres scoring the goals.

Summary:
Played: 8 Won: 5 Drawn: 3
Lost: 0 Goals for: 13
Goals against: 2

January 2021 was a superb month for the Blues who began the New Year with a blistering performance away to Chelsea.

Goals from Gundogan, Foden and De Bruyne blew Chelsea away at Stamford Bridge with the only surprise being City didn't win by more than the 3-1 final scoreline.

It looked like Guardiola's side had their spark back – and it was followed by an equally impressive 2-0 Carabao Cup semi-final win over Manchester United at Old Trafford to book a final spot with Spurs.

Birmingham were then dispatched 3-0 in the FA Cup before City recorded successive Premier League wins over Brighton, Crystal Palace and Aston Villa in the space of a week.

Cheltenham gave City a scare in the FA Cup third round, with the League Two side leading 1-0 up until the 81st-minute when a Foden-inspired comeback saw the Blues grab three goals in the time that remained.

An incredible January ended with two more Premier League wins: a 5-0 victory at West Brom and a narrow 1-0 home win over Sheffield United at the Etihad - making it 12 successive wins in all competitions.

Summary:
Played: 9 Won: 9 Drawn: 0
Lost: 0 Goals for: 24
Goals against: 2

FEBRUARY

If January had been special, February was perhaps even better.

City continued their winning streak with a 2-0 win at Burnley followed by a stunning 4-1 win away to Liverpool.

Despite missing a first-half penalty, Gundogan atoned by putting City ahead just after the re-start. Although Mo Salah then levelled, further goals from Gundogan, Foden and Sterling wrapped a huge victory for the Blues and a rare Anfield win. Progress continued in the FA Cup with a 3-1 win away to Swansea before City brushed Spurs aside 3-0 at the Etihad, Everton 3-1 at Goodison Park and Arsenal 1-0 at the Emirates – our 13th Premier League win in a row to put the Blues 10 points clear of Leicester at the top.

A comfortable 2-0 win over Borussia Monchengladbach in the Champions League Round of 16 first leg and a hard-fought 2-1 win over West Ham at the Etihad completed an incredible month for City who had now won 21 games in succession in all competitions.

Summary:
Played: 8 Won: 8 Drawn: 0
Lost: 0 Goals for: 20
Goals against: 4

MARCH

City's rich vein of form would continue during March, even though it would see an end to the winning streak.

A 4-1 win over Wolves at the Etihad edged City closer to the Premier League title, but Manchester United ended the long winning run that stretched back to early December by taking the Etihad derby 2-0.

City bounced back in style, though, thrashing Southampton 5-2 at home before beating Fulham 2-0 at Craven Cottage, putting Guardiola's men 17 points clear at the top of the table.

City eased into the UCL quarter-finals with a 2-0 second leg win against Borussia Monchengladbach, and late goals from Gundogan and De Bruyne secured a 2-0 win at Everton, booking an FA Cup semi-final berth for a side still gunning for a first-ever quadruple.

Summary:
Played: 6 Won: 5 Drawn: 0
Lost: 1 Goals for: 15
Goals against: 5

Summary:

Played: 7 Won: 5 Drawn: 0 Lost: 2 Goals for: 12 Goals against: 7

APRIL

City continued to steamroller towards the title with a 2-0 win away to Leicester at the start of April.

City then took on Borussia Dortmund in the first leg of the Champions League quarter-final. The Blues just edged home with a 2-1 win at the Etihad, but with Dortmund grabbing an away goal, the tie was finely poised.

That was followed by a surprise 2-1 home defeat to Leeds United, before the team travelled to face Dortmund. It was the Germans who went ahead first with a Jude Bellingham goal tipping the tie in their favour, but second-half goals from Mahrez and Foden ensured City's quarter-final curse didn't strike for a fourth year in a row, and the Blues moved into the semis for only the second time with a 4-2 aggregate win.

A much-changed City saw hopes of a quadruple ended at Wembley as Chelsea won the FA Cup semi-final 1-0, but there was just enough in the tank for City to beat Aston Villa 2-1 at Villa Park and move within a couple of wins of the title. The Blues then bagged the first trophy of the campaign when Aymeric Laporte's late header was enough to beat Tottenham 1-0 in the Carabao Cup final – our fourth success in that competition in a row!

An exhausting April ended with a superb 2-1 win away to Paris St Germain in the Champions League semi-final first leg, with De Bruyne and Mahrez putting City within 90 minutes of a first final.

There was still much for City to do in May, but it would prove to be a month of highs and lows.

It began with goals from Sergio Aguero and Torres putting City within one win of the title at Crystal Palace and was followed by an historic 2-0 second leg Champions League win over PSG.

It meant City would face Chelsea in the final for the very first time, with two Mahrez goals enough to see off the French champions. Ironically, City then faced Chelsea in the Premier League and having taken a 1-0 lead through Sterling, a penalty was then awarded a minute or so later. Aguero tried a Panenka style spot-kick which was saved easily, and the visitors came back to win 2-1.

The title was won without playing as Manchester United were beaten 2-1 at home by Leicester ensuring City were champions for the third time in four years.

A Torres hat-trick in an entertaining 4-3 win at Newcastle followed, and then City saw a 2-0 lead become a 3-2 defeat away to Brighton in the penultimate Premier League game of the campaign.

The final match proved a fairy-tale farewell for Club legend Aguero who climbed off the bench to score twice in a 5-0 thrashing of Everton – what a way to say goodbye by our all-time record goal-scorer!

Sadly, a magnificent campaign would end in heartbreak, as City lost the Champions League final 1-0 against Chelsea, with the Blues never really getting anywhere near our devastating best.

Still, what an incredible season!

Summary:
Played: 7 Won: 4 Drawn: 0 Lost: 3 Goals for: 16 Goals against: 9

STEPH HOUGHTON
Manchester City/England/Team GB

WORDSEARCH #1

See how many City men's team players you can find in our Wordsearch – remember, the words could be horizontal, vertical, diagonal or even backwards! There are 10 to find...

```
W R R O H N I D N A N R E F
T A B N K W D S R L H W P S
P E L M V M C E R D T K Z A
V D T K F L L R M G Z Y K I
M E Q W E T Y R Q Q G H Z D
P R Y V J R F O T D M D L K
Z S L P V V N T G P X H T F
L O S M T E L R R R H O C W
R N X E F F P K O K L T R N
D G J F N V V D X E Z Z M J
Q D E V W O R L C T F B C K
Q T K M L I T N J Y B B R M
S N C J G H A S P F O D E N
F X F O C C T W H M Y T Q M
```

TORRES **EDERSON** **DIAS**
STEFFEN **RODRIGO** **CANCELO**
FODEN **FERNANDINHO**
WALKER **STONES**

Jamaican goal-machine Khadija Shaw joined City from Bordeaux in the summer – here are 10 things you should know about our new striker...

1 BUNNY NICKNAME

Khadija is rarely called by her actual name – instead, everyone uses her nickname, 'Bunny'!

"I had it from when I was very small," she explains. "In Jamaican culture, you have your Sunday dinner – rice and peas with curried chicken or jerk chicken or fried chicken – and my mum would always make me carrot juice. From constantly wanting carrot juice, my brother gave me the name 'Bugs Bunny'.

"At the beginning, I hated it! He went and told all of his friends and all of my friends. It got really repetitive and one day, I thought: 'I'm going to embrace this name' and it's stuck ever since.

"Now, everybody calls me 'Bunny' but my brother is the only one who calls me 'Bugs'."

2 MANCHESTER TIES

"My dad's side of the family live in Manchester." Khadija reveals. "When I told them I'm going to come and play for City, they were so excited!

"I've heard about the rain, but I'm open! I've never been in a situation where it rains all the time so it will be a different experience … Playing in England is a great opportunity for me to go out and enjoy myself and have some fun!"

3 21

Shaw will wear the squad number 21 – a figure she believes is a special one.

"For me, 2021 has been a crazy year with the Coronavirus pandemic but also with how I've managed to develop, scoring 21 goals," she smiles.

"Having all the success that I'm having, I just think it's a year for me to remember and always look back on to say, 'This happened in 2021.'"

4 POLE POSITION

Prolific, tall and physical, Khadija says she models her game on Polish forward Robert Lewandowski, deeming her best attributes as her strength, dynamism in and around the box and willingness to put the team first.

"Attacking players are very exciting," she says. "I like Robert Lewandowski. I always watch him play. I think he's a great player. He plays in the same position I do and he's somebody I look up to.

"He's scored a lot of goals and I try to make his plays – the way he makes his runs – and that helps me."

5 WING WONDER

With 42 goals in 30 appearances, Shaw stands as her country's all-time record goal-scorer (in the male and female game) and has earned a reputation as one of the hottest offensive prospects in the world.

Although she is best-known as a number nine, she can also play on the wing – an exciting prospect given City's tendency to play with a potent attacking trio up top.

6 "BE YOURSELF"

Khadija's love of football began in the streets of her hometown. Although her mother raised concerns about whether her daughter should take part, Khadija's love for the game shone through and now she is now proud to be a role model to all young Caribbean boys and girls.

Khadija says the best piece of advice she has been given is simply: "to be yourself".

She says, "Never change for anyone. You're doing everything for you. At the end of the day, people are always going to talk; you can't make everyone happy in the world but you can make yourself happy."

7 A TRUE INSPIRATION

Khadija has achieved many great things at such a young age and her achievements are all the more impressive given the 24-year-old has overcome unimaginable personal tragedy.

She tragically lost four brothers and two nephews and has shown incredible mental strength and determination to go on to achieve her dreams.

Hailed for her 'remarkable' ability to 'overcome adversity, help others and set a sporting example', she was named The Guardian Footballer of the Year in 2018.

8 FOOD TO GO

Aside from family and friends (and probably the weather!), Khadija says the one other thing she will miss from back home in Jamaica is the food – jerk chicken in particular!

"You can go to another country and have similar food but the culture and the food and the background is something you definitely miss," she admits.

"Hopefully, when my family come to visit me in England, they can bring some with them!"

9 COMMUNICATION SKILLS

Shaw spent four years at college in America, studying and playing 'soccer' at Eastern Florida State and the University of Tennessee. She opted to study a degree in Communications to help her to overcome her shyness in interviews!

During her time in the States, she earned National Junior College Athletic Association All-America honours, was named in the All-SEC first team and was awarded SEC Offensive Player of the Year as a senior in 2018.

JACK GREALISH

It's fair to say that Jack Grealish is a player most football fans in England would like to have seen their club sign.

His receptions when playing for England during the delayed Euro 2020 tournament proved just how popular the Birmingham-born playmaker is and there was a growing clamour throughout the tournament to start him in games as he became the nation's new poster boy.

But it was City who activated Grealish's £100m release clause and brought him to the Etihad, much to the delight of City supporters young and old - but particularly the younger fans!

Grealish has built up a huge following of young fans in England with his instantly recognisable image, laidback nature and superb technical ability.

And with his boyband good looks, it is fair to say the Jack fan club stretches beyond the supporters of Manchester City!

So, what will our new signing bring to the team? The answer is plenty!

Though Pep Guardiola has said Jack can play in several positions, he was arguably at his most effective when playing on the left of a three-man attacking midfield trio.

At City, that could mean being alongside Kevin De Bruyne and Phil Foden, or playing as a more central No.10. Pep has even suggested he could play as a deep-lying centre-forward.

However, it is Jack's interplay that will work so well at City. He is at his most effective when he is central to the action, finding team-mates with clever passes, dribbling and drawing fouls in dangerous areas.

Over the past few seasons, he has been the most fouled player in the Premier League, because of his ability to shield the ball, his strength and the fact that the opposition are keen to get the ball off him as quickly as possible.

He became City's record signing when he joined the Club in the summer of 2021 - and in fact the first English player to cost £100million.

It was a huge wrench for Jack to leave his boyhood club Aston Villa, but the chance to play for City and be coached by Pep was too good to turn down. Jack wants to win trophies and he believes that by joining the most successful English club of the last decade, he will achieve his dreams at club and international level.

A fantastic signing who has quite rightly got the City fans very excited – welcome to Manchester, Jack!

FACTFILE:
JACK GREALISH

NAME: Jack Peter Grealish
DATE OF BIRTH: 10 September 1995
PLACE OF BIRTH: Birmingham, England
PREVIOUS CLUBS: Aston Villa, Notts County (on loan)
SQUAD NUMBER: 10
POSITION: Attacking midfielder
ENGLAND CAPS: 12*

(as of 1 September 2021)

8 QUESTIONS ON JACK

How much do you know about our new signing...?

1. TRUE OR FALSE? JACK MADE HIS SENIOR ASTON VILLA DEBUT AGAINST CITY.

....

....

2. WHICH CLUB DID JACK SPEND A SEASON ON LOAN WITH? BIRMINGHAM CITY, NOTTS COUNTY OR LEEDS UNITED?

....

....

3. WHO WORE THE NO.10 SHIRT AT CITY BEFORE JACK GREALISH?

....

....

4. JACK IS NOW AN ENGLAND PLAYER – BUT WHICH COUNTRY DID HE REPRESENT AT UNDER 17, 18 AND 21 LEVEL?
A) SCOTLAND B) REPUBLIC OF IRELAND OR C) NORTHERN IRELAND?

....

5. TRUE OR FALSE? JACK WEARS CHILD-SIZE SHINPADS WHEN HE PLAYS.

....

....

6. JACK WEARS HIS SOCKS ROLLED DOWN. IS THAT BECAUSE OF –
A) COMFORT B) STYLE C) SUPERSTITION?

....

7. AT WHAT AGE DID JACK FIRST JOIN ASTON VILLA?
A) 5 B) 6 C) 7

....

....

8. WHICH CITY PLAYER DID JACK STUDY TO IMPROVE HIS OWN GAME? A) SERGIO AGUERO B) PHIL FODEN C) KEVIN DE BRUYNE

....

....

Answers on page 60&61

JACK GREALISH
Manchester City/England

CARABAO CUP CHAMPIONS (AGAIN)!

City made it FOUR Carabao Cup successes in a row in 2020/21! Here are all the games and goals we scored along the way...

Round 3
City 2-1 Bournemouth

City began the defence of the Carabao Cup with a home tie against Championship side Bournemouth. It proved to be a trickier game than many expected but started well with teenager Liam Delap scoring a fine opening goal on his first-team debut. That put the Blues 1-0 up, but Sam Surridge levelled four minutes later for the Cherries who were causing the holders problems throughout. The winner came on 75 minutes through Phil Foden, ensuring City progressed to the last 16 of the competition.

Round 4
Burnley 0-3 City

City travelled the short distance to Turf Moor to take on Burnley in Round 4. It is a ground Pep Guardiola's side have had a lot of success on in recent years and this trip would be no different. The Clarets held out until the 35th-minute when Raheem Sterling finally broke the deadlock to put City 1-0 up at the break. And it was Sterling who bagged the Blues' second goal just four minutes into the second half, finishing from close range from Ferran Torres' low cross. Torres then completed the scoring with a well-taken third on 65 minutes as City eased into the quarter-finals.

Quarter-final
Arsenal 1-4 City

A trip to the Emirates presented a tough test for Guardiola's side but City were at their blistering best against the Gunners. Gabriel Jesus scored after just two minutes and City should have been out of sight before Alexandre Lacazette equalised for the hosts. But City shifted up another gear after the break with goals from Riyad Mahrez and Foden making it 3-1 before the hour-mark; and Aymeric Laporte wrapped up the victory on 73 minutes to seal a 4-1 win.

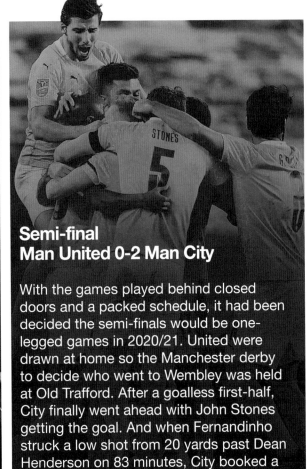

Semi-final
Man United 0-2 Man City

With the games played behind closed doors and a packed schedule, it had been decided the semi-finals would be one-legged games in 2020/21. United were drawn at home so the Manchester derby to decide who went to Wembley was held at Old Trafford. After a goalless first-half, City finally went ahead with John Stones getting the goal. And when Fernandinho struck a low shot from 20 yards past Dean Henderson on 83 minutes, City booked a place in the final against Tottenham.

Final
Spurs 0 Man City 1

City went into the game as favourites to make it four Carabao Cups in a row, but Tottenham were desperate to end their own long wait for a trophy. Spurs had sacked Jose Mourinho a few days before, but Guardiola ensured his team were focused on the job in hand. A small number of fans from both teams were allowed inside to watch the game, but it was the City supporters who were celebrating when Laporte's 82nd minute header from a Kevin De Bruyne cross proved to be the only goal, winning City the trophy on 1-0.

PLAYER OF THE YEAR 2020/21

The Player of the Season poll saw a record number of fan votes, with Ruben Dias being voted the worthy winner of City's best player for 2020/21.

The Portuguese centre-back, who was also named the 2021 Football Writers' Association Footballer of the Year and the Premier League Player of the Year, enjoyed a dream debut campaign, playing a crucial role in City's successes.

The 24-year-old signed from Benfica in September 2020 and was an integral cog in Pep Guardiola's relentless, record-breaking machine, making 50 appearances in total.

A commanding presence with a deep-rooted passion and strong winning mentality, Dias' influence has helped to seal a watertight defence, which last season conceded the fewest Premier League goals.

In addition to lifting the Premier League trophy and our fourth successive Carabao Cup, Dias was also part of the journey to a first Champions League final.

Asked how it felt to have won the award in his debut season, Dias expressed his gratitude to his teammates:

"I'M VERY PLEASED BUT I WON'T LET GO THE FACT THAT I'M ONLY HERE RECEIVING THIS BECAUSE WE WON THE PREMIER LEAGUE, THE CARABAO CUP AND WE'RE IN THE FINAL OF THE CHAMPIONS LEAGUE," HE SAID.

"BIG CREDIT GOES TO MY TEAMMATES, ESPECIALLY BECAUSE I'M A DEFENDER. FOR A DEFENDER TO WIN THIS, IT'S MAINLY BECAUSE OF THE TEAM. BIG THANKS TO ALL OF MY TEAMMATES.

"FOR A KID THAT BEFORE ALL OF IT WAS A FAN AND DREAMED OF BECOMING ONE OF THE STARS, I AM REALLY HAPPY TO BE HERE AND TO HAVE THE OPPORTUNITY TO PLAY WITH ALL THE GUYS I PLAY WITH IN MY TEAM."

"I AM REALLY HAPPY TO BE HERE AND TO HAVE THE OPPORTUNITY TO PLAY WITH ALL THE GUYS I PLAY WITH IN MY TEAM."

Dias was one of many City members to win awards last season – the others are listed in the column opposite:

TEAM AWARDS:

PFA Men's Team of the Year:
Included Ederson, Joao Cancelo, Ruben Dias, John Stones, Kevin De Bruyne and Ilkay Gundogan.

Women's Team of the Year
Included Caroline Weir, Sam Mewis, Lauren Hemp and Chloe Kelly.

INDIVIDUAL AWARDS:

Ruben Dias:
Voted Premier League Player of the Season, the Football Writer's Player of the Year and the Etihad Player of the Season.

Pep Guardiola:
Voted as both the Premier League and LMA Manager of the Year.

Kevin De Bruyne:
Voted the PFA Player of the Year for the second successive season, UEFA Midfielder of the Season in October 2020 and was part of the FIFPro 2019-2020 team of the year in December.

Phil Foden:
Voted both the PFA Young Player of the Year and Premier League Player of the Year

Ederson:
Retained the Premier League Golden Glove.

Lauren Hemp:
Voted PFA Women's Young Player of the Year for the second season running

Lucy Bronze:
Voted best women's player at FIFA's 2020 awards in December.

Men's Nissan Goal of the Season:
Ferran Torres (away vs Newcastle)

Women's Nissan Goal of the Season:
Caroline Weir (home to Manchester United)

SCM Player of the Season:
Chloe Kelly

Gatorade Rising Star award:
Esme Morgan

Premier League 2 Player of the Season:
Liam Delap

MAN CITY WOMEN

WOMEN

2020/21 SEASON REVIEW

Though it was an excellent campaign overall, Gareth Taylor's side would end the 2020/21 season without a trophy.

A thrilling FA Women's Super League campaign went all the way to the last game, with City unable to catch champions Chelsea despite winning 14 of the last 15 games.

The only match not won in that sequence was the one that would cost Taylor's side the title – a 2-2 draw with Chelsea at the CFA.

In fact, City would drop just 11 points from a possible 66 – five of those against Chelsea and costly early season slip-ups against Brighton and Reading proving to be the difference.

The pandemic meant the FA Cup campaign was suspended at the quarter-final stage and will be concluded during 2021/22, while the Continental Cup hopes were ended, once again, by Chelsea.

City's Champions League adventure saw victories over Goteborg and Fiorentina to set up a quarter-final with Barcelona Femmes.

A 3-0 defeat at a neutral location in Monza, Italy, was followed by a spirited 2-1 win at the Academy Stadium, but ultimately a defeat on aggregate.

At least City could take comfort from knowing we'd lost to the eventual winners of the competition with Barcelona beating (you guessed it) Chelsea 4-0 in the final.

Ellen White and Chloe Kelly top-scored in all competitions with 15 each and Sam Mewis bagged 14 goals. There were also impressive seasons for Lauren Hemp, Caroline Weir and Georgia Stanway, and no less than 10 of the City squad were selected for Team GB at the Tokyo Olympics in 2021.

With exciting new signings likely, Khadija Shaw among them, Taylor will be hoping his team can bring the silverware they deserve back to Manchester in 2021/22 – and with a skipper like Steph Houghton, everything is possible as our women's team goes from strength to strength.

GUESS WHO? #1

We have disguised four City men's team players with a mixture of pixelating and blurring. Use your knowledge and powers of observation to see if you can figure out who they are...

01

02

03

04

SPOT THE BALL #1

Can you spot the ball? We've removed the real ball from the picture below, so you have to figure out which grid square it should be in. It's tricky and maybe not as obvious as it first looks – Foden's face may offer a clue... or does it?!"

THE BIG CITY QUIZ 2022...

You will need all your City knowledge to crack our Big City Quiz which is tougher than ever! See how many you get right and then check your score.

01
Who was City's top scorer (all comps) in 2020/21?

02
Which was the only Etihad game where fans were allowed to attend in 2020/21?

03
Who did keeper Scott Carson make his debut against?

04
Which Academy player scored on his full senior debut?

05
Which Jamaican international joined City Women in the summer?

06
How many of our women's team were included in Team GB for the Tokyo Olympics?

07

True or false: Sergio Aguero came on as a sub and scored two goals in his first and last games at the Etihad.

08

Which City player was part of Wales' Euro 2020 squad?

09

Which of these is Phil Foden's favourite hobby – snooker, darts or fishing?

10

Which City player was awarded an MBE by the Queen in 2021?

11

Where was the Champions League final against Chelsea held – Budapest, Munich or Porto?

12

Who is the manager of Manchester City Women?

*Clue

13

True or False: Ederson holds the world record for the longest football drop kick.

14

Which of these clubs did Pep Guardiola NOT play for? Brescia, Roma or Club America

*Clue

15

Which team did Kyle Walker support as a boy?

16

Who did Ferran Torres score a Premier League hat-trick against?

17

Who were the only team to stop City scoring home and away last season?

18
Name one of the two City players who made 50 appearances last season.

19
What is Phil Foden's nickname?

20
Which team did Nathan Ake join City from?

21
What nationality is Caroline Weir?

22
How many points did City win the title by? 8, 10 or 12?

23
True or false: Marcus Rashford was once a City Academy player.

24
Which team did Club legend David Silva join in 2020?

25
Tommy Doyle's grandfathers both played for City – who were they?

26
Which team did Sergio Aguero join in 2021?

27
Which national team does goalkeeper Zack Steffen represent?

28
Six City players were named in the PFA Team of the Year – can you name four?

29
Who was the Etihad Player of the Season for 2020/21?

30
How many City players represented their country at Euro 2020? 10, 15 or 17

Clue

31
Which team were awarded **THREE** penalties against City at the Etihad in 2020/21?

32
Which City defender swapped France for Spain last season in time for the Euros?

33
Which League Two side led City in the FA Cup until nine minutes from time?

34
What is Phil Foden's squad number?

35
Who did Ferran Torres join City from?

36
Who did City and England captain Steph Houghton join City from?

*Clue

37
Who took David Silva's No.21 shirt in 2020/21?

38
What is Rodri's squad number?

39
Who won City's 2020/21 Goal of the Season vote?

40
Who won Manchester City Women's Goal of the Season?

SCORE:

10 POINTS OR LESS:
EXTRA TRAINING FOR YOU!

11-20 NOT BAD
YOU MIGHT GET A PLACE ON THE BENCH!

21-30:
SIGN A NEW CONTRACT NOW!

31-40:
YOU'VE GOT THE CAPTAIN'S ARMBAND - BRILLIANT!

Answers on page 61

GUESS WHO? #2

Here's your second helping of detective work to figure out which City men's team players are disguised below. The pictures were all taken after the Premier League trophy lift... but who are they?!

Answers on page 60&61

WORDSEARCH#2

There are 10 countries in the wordsearch below that relate to our current players – they are hidden in the wordsearch below – horizontal, vertical, backwards… see how many you can find!

```
T V U N C T M T Z H P L H M
S D N A L R E H T E N Z P J
N A I P M L P M L L R W W G
Z I T D V U H O I T Y Y K F
G R E Y W H I Z R T Z M L X
K E D Y B Q A G W T Q L K V
Y G S D R R G E L M U F D U
H L T N B J W R F E W G K K
V A A A M Y Y M T K B R A B
N L T L J W W A T X A J M L
F V E G R W W N D I R M T X
T J S N L F N Y N V D M J X
Z M N E G R M E X J M Y J R
P K K M M M H S P A I N M Y
```

ENGLAND   **GERMANY**   **BELGIUM**
BRAZIL   **UNITED STATES**   **ALGERIA**
SPAIN   **UKRAINE**
PORTUGAL   **NETHERLANDS**

Answers on page 60&61

GABRIEL JESUS
Manchester City/Brazil

RAHEEM STERLING
Manchester City/England

I WANNA BE...
PHIL FODEN

Phil Foden is one of the most exciting homegrown talents City have ever had - a boyhood blue living the dream. But how can you follow in his footsteps? Here's our guide to help you try and be like Foden by doing some of the things he did on his journey to City's first team...

JOIN A LOCAL CLUB

Joining a local junior football team is a great way to start regular training and to learn the basics of football.

You'll improve your fitness, get used to a routine, understand technique and how to improve it, as well as taking part in junior short-sided matches.

Phil joined Reddish Vulcans in Stockport aged 7 and represented Reddish Tornadoes to begin with.

Playing for a club will help you discover your best position (though this may change over time as your development progresses) and get you used to being part of a team.

It doesn't cost too much in weekly subsidies, though there is usually an initial joining fee which will cover the cost of your training gear and football kit.

PRACTISE, PRACTISE, PRACTISE

It is often said that Phil Foden plays and trains as though he was with his friends at school.

His energy and enthusiasm come from a natural love of football, but it also comes from dedication.

Phil would play football whenever he could – in the garden, in the park or in the street.

If your dream is to become a professional footballer, you will have to put a lot of hard work and dedication in to achieve your goal.

EAT WELL, SLEEP WELL

Getting plenty of sleep is important for everybody, but especially if you are going to school, doing homework, and training or playing regularly.

Knowing when to get rest and relax is important – that means knowing when to stop playing on your Xbox and turn off your phone if you have either!

Eating the right foods at the right time is also key – there is plenty of online nutritional advice for all ages, but plenty of fruit, vegetables and having a healthy balanced diet is crucial for any young person.

Fizzy drinks and too much sugar in your diet is not the way forward, though in moderation, it's OK to have occasional treats!

TRAINING

Listen to your coaches and work hard. Players who stand around talking and not listening will miss useful information that might improve their game.

Work hard at every session – it is for your own benefit. Phil Foden would finish training sessions then go back and train a bit more on his own or with friends. He still does this with England!

STUDY THE BEST

If you want to be like Phil Foden or any top footballer, watch clips of how they play and what they do.

If you are a defender, watch how your heroes play. If you are a striker, watch top strikers and how they move and make runs or space during matches. Take notes.

There are many players who have inspired Phil – David Silva being perhaps the most influential – but while he learned some of how Silva played, Phil always liked to have his own style and not copy anyone else.

So observe, absorb and adapt to your strengths, but play the way that is best for you.

KNOW YOUR WEAKNESSES

Every player has weaknesses in their game – things they wish they were better at.

Phil is left-footed so he practises a lot using his right foot – he recognises he can be better by improving his right foot more, so he keeps trying to get better and better.

Identify any weaknesses in your game and practise continually to become stronger in that area – it will improve your all-round game and potentially make you a more flexible player for the squad.

ENJOY IT!

It takes a lot of work and talent to become a professional footballer. Although only a handful make it, it doesn't mean you can't be one of them.

Phil joined City's Academy after he was spotted playing for his local club. He was even a ball-boy at the Etihad so maybe join the Junior Cityzens and see if there are competitions to be a ball-boy or ball-girl.

But if you're not one of the lucky few, it should never stop you from playing and enjoying football.

It is a wonderful game with many positive benefits and you will be able to play for many years, whether that's with a professional club, amateur club, at five-a-side or just in the park with your pals.

You can bet that if Phil Foden hadn't made it with City, he'd probably be out playing most days of the week just because he loves the game.

Australian forward Hayley Raso joined City in the summer...

Australian international Hayley Raso joined City during the summer of 2021 after agreeing a two-year deal.

Born in Brisbane, the Aussie forward spent the previous 18 months with Everton, helping them reach the Women's FA Cup final, as well as a fifth-place finish in the FA Women's Super League.

Raso is an exciting and versatile player capable of playing as a striker or as a winger – though she's opted for the unusual squad number of two – usually associated more with a right-back!

Prior to her switch to Everton in January 2020, the 26-year-old had played for Australian sides Canberra United, Brisbane Roar and Melbourne Victory, alongside stints in the United States with Washington Spirit (2015) and Portland Thorns FC (2016-2019).

Raso won W-League titles with Brisbane and Canberra, and was successful with Portland, securing the NWSL Championship and Shield during her time in the States as well as being named as Rose City Riveters' Most Valuable Player in 2017.

At international level, Raso's CV is even more impressive!

She has represented Australia – also known as the 'Matildas' - at senior level since 2012 and to date has earned more than 50 caps, helping them to Tournament of Nations and FFA Cup of Nations successes in 2017 and 2019 respectively.

But it's not all been smooth running for our new forward - on 25 August 2018 while playing for Portland, Raso fractured three vertebrae in her back in a nasty collision that involved a knee in her back.

Not only was Raso's career in doubt, she was unsure if she would ever walk again, such was the seriousness of the injury. Luckily, thanks to expert medical help and her own grit and determination, she made a full recovery and six months later, returned to competitive football.

With that fighting spirit, she is a welcome addition to Gareth Taylor's squad for the 2021/22.

5 THINGS YOU NEED TO KNOW ABOUT...

HAYLEY RASO

• Hayley represented Australia in the 2020 Olympic Games and was part of the Aussie side that eliminated a Team GB side that included eight future City team-mates in a thrilling 4-3 win.

• Hayley wears ribbons in her hair to match the colour of the team she is representing – sent by her grandmother in Australia!

• She is very superstitious! She turns her socks inside out before each game – then always puts the left on before the right!

• She has a tattoo on her foot that says 'Don't look back, leave it on the track' – a motto her mum instilled in her at an early age...

•Hayley became a footballer because of her older brother's love of the sport.

NAME GAME

See if you can work out which eight City players are contained within the anagrams below – it may look like a random collection of words, but there is a player in there somewhere!

1. RED NOSE

2. NO NO H JESTS

3. E BUY DRINK EVEN

4. POLE TRY AMERICA

5. RHYME IZ DARE

6. AN US BRIDE

7. IF HEN PLOD

8. REF ROARS RENT

Answers on page 60&61

JOHN STONES
Manchester City/England

Spain international midfielder Vicky Losada joined City ahead of the new 2021/22 season.

1 WINNING NUMBERS

Losada has opted to wear the number 17 shirt ahead of her debut season for City.

She revealed that she chose that particular number so that she could emulate her counterpart in the men's team: PFA Player of the Year, Kevin De Bruyne.

2 TERRIFIC TREBLE

Last season saw Barcelona, captained by Losada, in a display of utter dominance. Not only did they claim a historic treble, including the biggest prize in European football, they would do so having lost just two matches in all competitions. Their season culminated in a 4-0 Champions League final victory over WSL Champions, Chelsea.

3 TOUGH OPPONENTS

While Barcelona ultimately came out on top in our UEFA Women's Champions League quarter-final, Losada believes Manchester City gave them their toughest test of the 2020/21 campaign:

"In my opinion, City were the best team we played against last year," she revealed.

She also feels that, of all those competing in the WSL, she can draw the most comparisons between her former employers and Gareth Taylor's side.

"In my experience, the hardest games were when teams used to play like us, and if I had to compare Barca with any team in England now, it would definitely be Manchester City."

4 PUPPY LOVE

Losada's energy in the middle of the park will prove vital for City next season and, given she has to keep pace with two dogs in her spare time, it's clear to see where she gets it from!

"I have two dogs, and I love them," she beamed when asked about what she does in her spare time.

"They're so much work! I have a Shiba Inu and a Border Collie mixed with a German Shepherd - that girl is the one who wakes me up every morning, rolling around with her!"

5 HISTORY MAKER

Losada broke new ground on an international front when she found the back of the net in the 2015 Women's World Cup against Costa Rica.

Although Spain would ultimately fail to qualify for the knockout rounds, that summer's World Cup represented their first appearance in the full competition.

As such, the midfielder's strike in La Roja's opening game means she holds the distinction of being her nation's first ever World Cup goal-scorer.

6 HOME FROM HOME

Vicky has already played in England courtesy of a two-season stint at Arsenal between 2015 and 2016. While Barcelona will of course always be in her heart, Losada is delighted to return to a league where she feels she reached the peak of her powers.

The midfielder admitted the competitiveness of the English game has always been a massive draw for her.

She reflected: "I think my best time was in England, 100%. I miss the game, the competitiveness, the game in England is faster and you can lose or win against any team. I missed that kind of war feeling every weekend."

7 PEP TALK

Given her position, it perhaps comes as no surprise that growing up in Catalonia during the 1990s, Losada's first footballing idol was none other than current City boss, Pep Guardiola.

"When I was younger I watched men's football," she recalled. "My first player was Pep Guardiola, but I don't have many memories because I was very young! It then became Andres Iniesta and Xavi [who I followed]."

8 AMERICAN DREAM

The Spanish midfielder enjoyed a brief stint across the Atlantic Ocean, swapping Barcelona for National Women's Soccer League team, Western New York Flash in February 2014.

She immediately hit the ground running, grabbing two goals and an assist on her debut to be voted NWSL player of the week.

9 THE FUTURE'S BRIGHT

The Women's game has grown exponentially in recent decades, and Vicky is hopeful that she can have a positive impact on future generations looking to make it in the beautiful game.

"I think it's very important to have role models in women's football," she pointed out. "They can see themselves reflected in us, and they can start when they're very young having dreams of winning the Champions League and being a professional footballer.

"It's something I never had [a female footballing role model], and I think it's a massive change that is going to make women's football even better."

WHOSE BOOTS?

Can you guess who the boots in the pictures below belong to?

01

02

03

04

Answers on page 60&61

SPOT THE BALL #2

Here's our second Spot the Ball puzzle – we've added a grid to make it slightly easier – but which box is the ball in? Check the players' eyes and body language to see if you can figure where Riyad Mahrez's shot is heading...

Answers on page 60&61

CITY LEGENDS HONOURED FOREVER...

The first statues in honour of Manchester City players were unveiled just before the 2021/22 season began.

In recognition of the incredible service given by City legends Vincent Kompany and David Silva, the Club considered a number of ways that supporters could remember their heroes.

Eventually, it was decided that permanent monuments outside the Etihad Stadium were the ideal way of ensuring both players would never be far from their spiritual home of Manchester.

City skipper Vincent Kompany made 360 appearances for the Club and became our most successful captain of all time, winning 12 trophies in sky blue. The inspirational Belgian left in 2019, but his legacy will never be forgotten.

David Silva, nicknamed 'El Mago' – The Magician – was one of the most popular players to ever represent Manchester City. In his 10 years at the Etihad, he played 436 games and scored 77 goals – winning 14 trophies with the Club to become our most successful player of all time.

While Kompany's leadership inspired the players and fans, Silva's skill, vision and brilliance lit up the Etihad for a decade.

Both Kompany and Silva were recognised as two of the most influential overseas signings the Premier League has ever seen and they were – and remain – Manchester City legends.

The statues were commissioned by City in 2020, with renowned sculptor Andy Scott chosen to create them. Scott has created

more than 80 contemporary projects, which can be found both in the UK and in many corners of the world. He worked on the City players' tribute from his studio in the USA.

By the start of the 2021/22 campaign, the statues had been transported to Manchester and were unveiled before the home game against Arsenal.

City Chairman, Khaldoon Al Mubarak commented:
"Ultimately, Vincent and David do not need statues to enshrine their achievements at Manchester City over the past decade. They are already revered as icons of their generation.

"But what these artworks give us, and generations to come, is the opportunity to be reminded of, and savour, the truly magical moments created by both men."

And next summer, City will unveil a third statue – this one of our all-time record goal-scorer Sergio Aguero who will also be honoured with a permanent monument at the Etihad.

To see the statues at the Etihad, visit the East Stand when you are at a game or in Manchester!

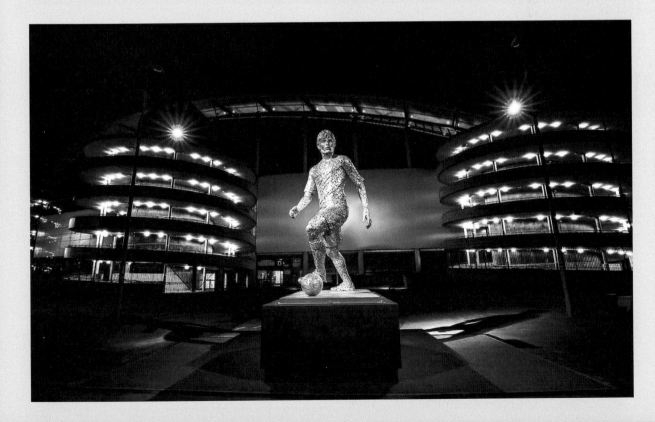

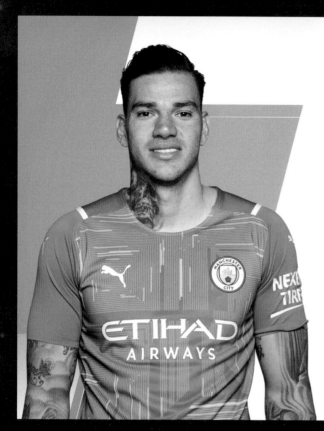

NAME: EDERSON MORAES
POSITION: GOALKEEPER
SQUAD NUMBER: 31
DATE OF BIRTH: 17/08/1993
PREVIOUS CLUBS: RIO AVE, BENFICA
TOTAL CITY CAREER:
PLAYED: 191 GOALS: 0

NAME: ZACK STEFFEN
POSITION: GOALKEEPER
SQUAD NUMBER: 13
DATE OF BIRTH: 02/04/1995
PREVIOUS CLUBS: SC FREIBURG II, COLUMBUS CREW, FORTUNA DUSSELDORF (LOAN)
TOTAL CITY CAREER:
PLAYED: 12 GOALS: 0

NAME: SCOTT CARSON
POSITION: GOALKEEPER
SQUAD NUMBER: 33
DATE OF BIRTH: 03/09/1985
PREVIOUS CLUBS: LEEDS,
LIVERPOOL, SHEFF WEDS (LOAN),
CHARLTON (LOAN), ASTON VILLA
(LOAN), WEST BROM, BURSASPOR,
DERBY (LOAN), WIGAN, DERBY,
MANCHESTER CITY (LOAN)
TOTAL CITY CAREER:
PLAYED: 1 GOALS: 0

NAME: KYLE WALKER
POSITION: RIGHT-BACK
SQUAD NUMBER: 2
DATE OF BIRTH: 28/05/1990
PREVIOUS CLUBS: SHEFFIELD
UNITED, NORTHAMPTON (LOAN),
SPURS, SHEFFIELD UNITED (LOAN),
QPR (LOAN), ASTON VILLA (LOAN)
TOTAL CITY CAREER:
PLAYED: 184 GOALS: 5

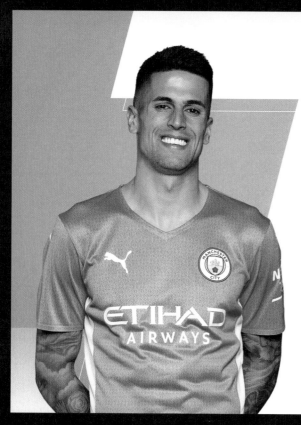

NAME: JOAO CANCELO
POSITION: RIGHT-BACK
SQUAD NUMBER: 27
DATE OF BIRTH: 27/05/1994
PREVIOUS CLUBS: BENFICA B, BENFICA, VALENCIA, INTER MILAN, JUVENTUS
TOTAL CITY CAREER:
PLAYED: 76 GOALS: 4

NAME: JOHN STONES
POSITION: CENTRAL DEFENDER
SQUAD NUMBER: 5
DATE OF BIRTH: 28/05/1994
PREVIOUS CLUBS: BARNSLEY, EVERTON
TOTAL CITY CAREER:
PLAYED: 168 GOALS: 10

NAME: RUBEN DIAS
POSITION: CENTRAL DEFENDER
SQUAD NUMBER: 3
DATE OF BIRTH: 14/05/1997
PREVIOUS CLUBS: BENFICA B, BENFICA
TOTAL CITY CAREER:
PLAYED: 50 GOALS: 1

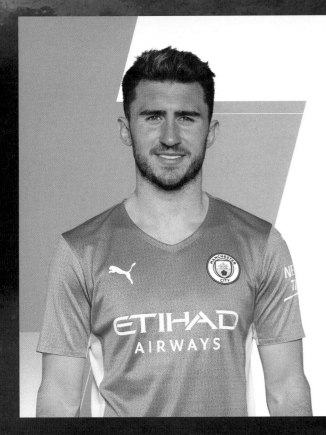

NAME: AYMERIC LAPORTE
POSITION: CENTRAL DEFENDER
SQUAD NUMBER: 14
DATE OF BIRTH: 27/05/1994
PREVIOUS CLUBS: BASCONIA, BILBAO ATHLETIC, ATHLETIC BILBAO
TOTAL CITY CAREER:
PLAYED: 111 GOALS: 8

NAME: OLEKSANDR ZINCHENKO
POSITION: LEFT-BACK
SQUAD NUMBER: 11
DATE OF BIRTH: 15/12/1996
PREVIOUS CLUBS: UFA, PSV, JONG PSV
TOTAL CITY CAREER:
PLAYED: 100 GOALS: 2

NAME: NATHAN AKE
POSITION: DEFENDER
SQUAD NUMBER: 6
DATE OF BIRTH: 18/02/1995
PREVIOUS CLUBS: CHELSEA, WATFORD (LOAN), READING (LOAN), BOURNEMOUTH (LOAN), BOURNEMOUTH
TOTAL CITY CAREER:
PLAYED: 13 GOALS: 1

NAME: RODRIGO
POSITION: DEFENSIVE MIDFIELDER
SQUAD NUMBER: 16
DATE OF BIRTH: 22/06/1994
PREVIOUS CLUBS: VILLARREAL B, VILLARREAL, ATHLETICO MADRID
TOTAL CITY CAREER:
PLAYED: 105 GOALS: 6

NAME: BERNARDO SILVA
POSITION: ATTACKING MIDFIELDER
SQUAD NUMBER: 20
DATE OF BIRTH: 10/08/1994
PREVIOUS CLUBS: BENFICA, MONACO
TOTAL CITY CAREER:
PLAYED: 201 GOALS: 35

NAME: FERNANDINHO
POSITION: MIDFIELDER
SQUAD NUMBER: 25
DATE OF BIRTH: 04/05/1985
PREVIOUS CLUBS: ATLÉTICO PARANAENSE, SHAKHTAR DONETSK
TOTAL CITY CAREER:
PLAYED: 350 GOALS: 24

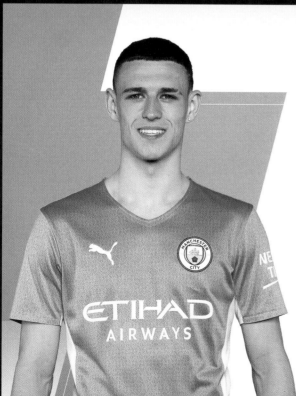

NAME: PHIL FODEN
POSITION: MIDFIELDER
SQUAD NUMBER: 47
DATE OF BIRTH: 28/05/2000
PREVIOUS CLUBS: ACADEMY GRADUATE
TOTAL CITY CAREER:
PLAYED: 124 GOALS: 31

NAME: ILKAY GUNDOGAN
POSITION: MIDFIELDER
SQUAD NUMBER: 8
DATE OF BIRTH: 24/10/1990
PREVIOUS CLUBS: VFL BOCHUM, FC NURNBERG, BORUSSIA DORTMUND
TOTAL CITY CAREER:
PLAYED: 210 GOALS: 39

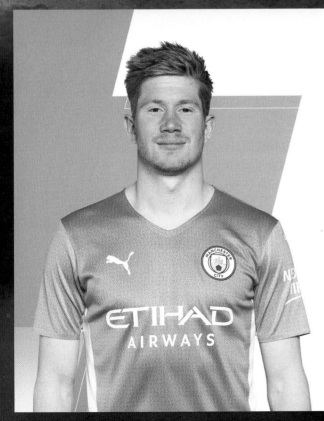

NAME: KEVIN DE BRUYNE
POSITION: ATTACKING MIDFIELDER
SQUAD NUMBER: 17
DATE OF BIRTH: 28/06/1991
PREVIOUS CLUBS: GENK, CHELSEA, WERDER BREMEN (LOAN), WOLFSBURG
TOTAL CITY CAREER:
PLAYED: 262 GOALS: 67

NAME: RIYAD MAHREZ
POSITION: ATTACKING MIDFIELDER
SQUAD NUMBER: 26
DATE OF BIRTH: 21/02/1991
PREVIOUS CLUBS: QUIMPER, LE HAVRE, LE HAVRE, LEICESTER CITY
TOTAL CITY CAREER:
PLAYED: 142 GOALS: 39

NAME: RAHEEM STERLING
POSITION: WINGER
SQUAD NUMBER: 7
DATE OF BIRTH: 08/12/1994
PREVIOUS CLUBS: QPR, LIVERPOOL
TOTAL CITY CAREER:
PLAYED: 292 GOALS: 114

NAME: GABRIEL JESUS
POSITION: STRIKER
SQUAD NUMBER: 9
DATE OF BIRTH: 03/04/1997
PREVIOUS CLUBS: PALMEIRAS
TOTAL CITY CAREER:
PLAYED: 195 GOALS: 82

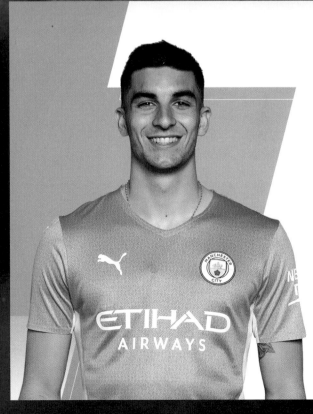

NAME: FERRAN TORRES
POSITION: WINGER
SQUAD NUMBER: 21
DATE OF BIRTH: 29/02/2000
PREVIOUS CLUBS: VALENCIA B,
VALENCIA
TOTAL CITY CAREER:
PLAYED: 36 GOALS: 13

QUIZ AND PUZZLE *ANSWERS*

WORDSEARCH#1
(From page 15)

```
W R R O H N I D N A N R E F
T A B N K W D S R L H W P S
P E L M V M C E R D T K Z A
V D T K F L L R M G Z Y K I
M E Q W E T Y R Q Q G H Z D
P R Y V J R F O T D M D L K
Z S L P V V N T G P X H T F
L O S M T E L R R R H O C W
R N X E F F P K O K L T R N
D G J F N V D X E Z Z M J
Q D E V W O R L C T F B C K
Q T K M L I T N J Y B B R M
S N C J G H A S P F O D E N
F X F O C C T W H M Y T Q M
```

WORDSEARCH#2
(From page 35)

```
T V U N C T M T Z H P L H M
S D N A L R E H T E N Z P J
N A I P M L P M L L R W W G
Z I T D V U H O I T Y Y K F
G R E Y W H I Z R T Z M L X
K E D Y B Q A G W T Q L K V
Y G S D R R G E L M U F D U
H L T N B J W R F E W G K K
V A A M Y Y M T K B R A B
N L T L J W W A T X A J M L
F V E G R W W N D I R M T X
T J S N L F N Y N V D M J X
Z M N E G R M E X J M Y J R
P K K M M M H S P A I N M Y
```

GUESS WHO?#1
(From page 28)

01 RODRIGO
02 GABRIEL JESUS

03 JOAO CANCELO
04 RUBEN DIAS

SPOT THE BALL#1 (From page 29)

SPOT THE BALL#2 (From page 47)

GUESS WHO?#2
(From page 34)

01 FERRAN TORRES

02 JOHN STONES

03 KEVIN DE BRUYNE
04 OLEKSANDR ZINCHENKO

8 QUESTIONS ON GREALISH (From page 20)

1. TRUE – IN 2014
2. NOTTS COUNTY
3. SERGIO AGUERO
4. B - REPUBLIC OF IRELAND
5. TRUE!
6. C - SUPERSTITION
7. B - SIX
8. C - DE BRUYNE

NAME GAME ANSWERS (From page 42)

1. EDERSON
2. JOHN STONES
3. KEVIN DE BRUYNE
4. AYMERIC LAPORTE
5. RIYAD MAHREZ
6. RUBEN DIAS
7. PHIL FODEN
8. FERRAN TORRES

WHOSE BOOTS (From page 46)

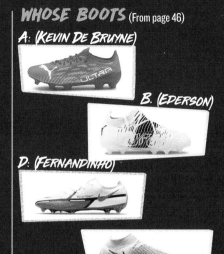

A: (KEVIN DE BRUYNE)

B. (EDERSON)

D: (FERNANDINHO)

C: (RUBEN DIAS)

THE BIG CITY QUIZ 2022 (From page 30-33)

1. ILKAY GUNDOGAN (17)
2. VERSUS EVERTON IN MAY
3. NEWCASTLE UNITED AWAY
4. LIAM DELAP
5. KHADIJA SHAW
6. 10
7. TRUE – V SWANSEA 2011 AND EVERTON 2021
8. MATT SMITH
9. FISHING
10. RAHEEM STERLING
11. PORTO
12. GARETH TAYLOR
13. TRUE!
14. CLUB AMERICA
15. SHEFFIELD UNITED
16. NEWCASTLE
17. MANCHESTER UNITED
18. RUBEN DIAS OR PHIL FODEN
19. THE STOCKPORT INIESTA
20. BOURNEMOUTH
21. SCOTTISH
22. 12 POINTS
23. FALSE
24. REAL SOCIEDAD
25. MIKE DOYLE AND GLYN PARDOE
26. BARCELONA
27. USA
28. EDERSON, JOAO CANCELO, RUBEN DIAS, JOHN STONES, KEVIN DE BRUYNE AND ILKAY GUNDOGAN WERE ALL INCLUDED.
29. RUBEN DIAS
30. 15
31. LEICESTER CITY
32. AYMERIC LAPORTE
33. CHELTENHAM TOWN
34. 47
35. VALENCIA
36. ARSENAL
37. FERRAN TORRES
38. NO. 16
39. FERRAN TORRES V NEWCASTLE AWAY
40. CAROLINE WEIR V MANCHESTER UNITED HOME

WHERE'S KEVIN?

Our brilliant Belgian Kevin De Bruyne is somewhere among the City fans at Wembley – your job is to find him! Warning – you made need a magnifying glass...